Mixing Colours with

White

Vic Parker

Heinemann
LIBRARY

Little Nippers

www.heinemann.co.uk/library
Visit our website to find out more information about **Heinemann Library** books.

To order:
☎ Phone 44 (0) 1865 888066
▤ Send a fax to 44 (0) 1865 314091
▯ Visit the Heinemann bookshop at www.heinemann.co.uk/library to browse our catalogue and order online.

First published in Great Britain by Heinemann Library, Halley Court, Jordan Hill, Oxford OX2 8EJ, part of Harcourt Education. Heinemann is a registered trademark of Harcourt Education Ltd.

Editorial: Jilly Attwood and Claire Throp
Design: Jo Hinton-Malivoire and Tipani Design (www.tipani.co.uk)
Models made by: Jo Brooker
Picture Research: Rosie Garai and Sally Smith
Production: Séverine Ribierre

Originated by Dot Gradations
Printed and bound in China by South China Printing Company

ISBN 0 431 17343 5 (hardback)
08 07 06 05 04
10 9 8 7 6 5 4 3 2 1

ISBN 0 431 17348 6 (paperback)
08 07 06 05 04
10 9 8 7 6 5 4 3 2 1

British Library Cataloguing in Publication Data
Parker, Vic
Mixing Colours with white
752
A full catalogue record for this book is available from the British Library.

Acknowledgements
The publishers would like to thank Trevor Clifford for permission to reproduce the photographs in this book.

Cover photograph reproduced with permission of Trevor Clifford.

The publishers would like to thank Annie Davy for her assistance in the preparation of this book.

Every effort has been made to contact copyright holders of any material reproduced in this book. Any omissions will be rectified in subsequent printings if notice is given to the publishers.

The paper used to print this book comes from sustainable resources.

Contents

The colour white

All of these are white.

Which would you choose to make a white picture?

What is white?

What can you think of that is white?

White and green

Adding white makes a
colour lighter.

Pale minty-green paint is perfect for a creepy crawly caterpillar.

White and red

red strawberry juice

white milk

slurp! slurp!

slurp!

pink strawberry
milkshake

Yum, yum!

11

White and purple

Count the pale purple prints.

Pale purple is sometimes called lilac or mauve.

White and blue

A little white, a **lot** of blue.

Can you see the pale blue footprints too?

15

White and yellow!

white sugar

yellow colouring

16

White and black

White-and-black or
black-and-white?

18

Do you know what colour you get if you mix them together?

grey

paler and paler

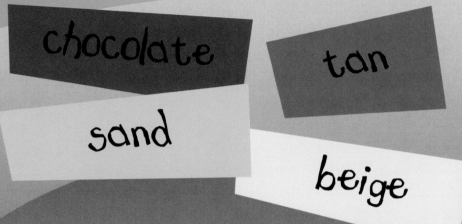

chocolate

tan

sand

beige

When brown is made
whiter and **whiter** and **whiter**,

it becomes
lighter and **lighter** and **lighter**.

Count the tints

If you add **lots** of white paint to other paint colours you get pretty pastel colours.

Can you name them all?

Index

The end

Notes for adults

The *Mixing Colours* series explores what happens when you blend two colours (occasionally three) together. The books focus on the mixing of pure paint colours, while also leading children to think about other pigments, such as crayons, chalks, pens and dyes. There are four titles in the series, focusing on the primary colours and white. Used together, the books will help enable children to differentiate between colours and begin to understand how they are made. They can also be used to encourage children to talk about what happens when colours are mixed, using appropriate language such as lighter, darker and shade. The following Early Learning Goals are relevant to this series:
Creative development
Early learning goals for exploring media and materials:
• explore what happens when they mix colours
• understand that different media can be combined.

This book encourages young children to explore what happens when they mix white with other colours, and invites them to experiment with the resulting different shades to make paintings, drawings, collages, constructions, masks and models, etc. The book will help children extend their vocabulary, as they will hear new words such as *mauve* and *beige*.

Follow-up activities
• See how many white objects your child can find around the house. Draw or paint a picture of a snowman, chef (in white uniform and hat) or zebra on a blackboard or sheet of black paper.
• Cut sheets of newspaper into strips. Make pale paints by adding white to other colours. Paint the strips, leave them to dry, and then glue them into a paper chain to decorate the room.
• Bake or buy some fairy cakes. Add drops of blue, red and yellow food colouring to icing sugar to make pale, pastel-coloured icing for the cakes.